G. Music Theory Multiple Choice Exercise

(Based on ABRSM Grade 4

Music Theory Syllabus

from 2020 onwards)

Regina Pratley

DEDICATION

Dedicated to those who are going to take the ABRSM
grade 4 Music Theory exam from 2020 onwards.

CONTENTS

	Introduction	i
1	Time Signatures	3
2	Shift between simple time and compound time	7
3	Rewrite a bar of notes:	17
	twice the value or half the value	
4	Grouping	27
5	Rests	37
6	Concept of note values	45
7	Enharmonic equivalent	47
8	Concept of pitch	57
9	Keys	72
10	Scales	81
11	Technical names	101
12	Intervals	104
13	Triads/ Chords	113
14	Terms, Signs and Instruments	126
	Answer Keys	140

INTRODUCTION

The ABRSM grade 4 Music Theory exam will take place online from 2020 onwards! Nearly all of the questions will become multiple choices questions, though some of them may still need you to write simple answers (e.g. write a number or draw a note). Therefore, students have to get used to the new format of the exam.

This book is written for students who are going to take the grade 4 Music Theory exam in new format. Hope you all will find it easier and get used to it soon! ☺

Chapter 1
Time Signatures

1. Circle the correct time signature for the following bar.

$\frac{6}{4}$ C $\frac{3}{2}$

2. Circle the correct time signature for the following bar.

C $\frac{6}{4}$ $\frac{9}{8}$

3. Circle the correct time signature for the following bar.

$$\frac{9}{4} \qquad \frac{4}{2} \qquad \frac{3}{2}$$

4. Circle the correct time signature for the following bar.

$$\frac{9}{16} \qquad \frac{6}{8} \qquad \frac{12}{16}$$

5. Circle the correct time signature for the following bar.

$$\frac{3}{4} \qquad \frac{4}{4} \qquad \frac{6}{8}$$

6. Circle the correct time signature for the following bar.

$\frac{9}{8}$ $\frac{6}{8}$ $\frac{3}{4}$

7. Circle the correct time signature for the following bar.

$\frac{9}{8}$ $\frac{6}{4}$ $\frac{12}{8}$

8. Circle the correct time signature for the following bar.

$\frac{6}{4}$ $\frac{4}{4}$ $\frac{3}{2}$

9. Circle the correct time signature for the following bar.

$$\frac{12}{8} \qquad\qquad \frac{9}{4} \qquad\qquad \frac{4}{2}$$

10. Circle the correct time signature for the following bar.

$$\frac{9}{16} \qquad\qquad \frac{6}{8} \qquad\qquad \frac{12}{16}$$

Chapter 2
Shift between simple time and compound time.

1. Here is a bar in simple time.

Which of the following shows the bar above correctly rewritten in compound time? Circle the correct answer.

A

B

C

2. Here is a bar in simple time.

Which of the following shows the bar above correctly rewritten in compound time? Circle the correct answer.

3. Here is a bar in simple time.

Which of the following shows the bar above correctly rewritten in compound time? Circle the correct answer.

4. Here is a bar in simple time.

Which of the following shows the bar above correctly rewritten in compound time? Circle the correct answer.

5. Here is a bar in simple time.

Which of the following shows the bar above correctly rewritten in compound time? Circle the correct answer.

6. Here is a bar in compound time.

Which of the following shows the bar above correctly rewritten in simple time? Circle the correct answer.

7. Here is a bar in compound time.

Which of the following shows the bar above correctly rewritten in simple time? Circle the correct answer.

8. Here is a bar in compound time.

Which of the following shows the bar above correctly rewritten in simple time? Circle the correct answer.

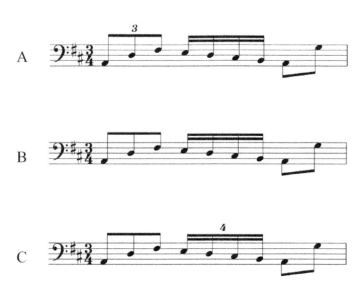

9. Here is a bar in compound time.

Which of the following shows the bar above correctly rewritten in simple time? Circle the correct answer.

10. Here is a bar in compound time.

Which of the following shows the bar above correctly rewritten in simple time? Circle the correct answer.

Chapter 3

Rewrite a bar of notes:

twice the value or half the value

1. Look at the following bar.

Which of the following is correctly rewritten in **twice the value** of the bar above? Circle the correct answer.

A

B

C

2. Look at the following bar.

Which of the following is correctly rewritten in **half the value** of the bar above? Circle the correct answer.

3. Look at the following bar.

Which of the following is correctly rewritten in **twice the value** of the bar above? Circle the correct answer.

4. Look at the following bar.

Which of the following is correctly rewritten in **half the value** of the bar above? Circle the correct answer.

A

B

C

5. Look at the following bar.

Which of the following is correctly rewritten in **twice the value** of the bar above? Circle the correct answer.

A

B

C

6. Look at the following bar.

Which of the following is correctly rewritten in **twice the value** of the bar above? Circle the correct answer.

A

B

C

7. Look at the following bar.

Which of the following is correctly rewritten in **half the value** of the bar above? Circle the correct answer.

8. Look at the following bar.

Which of the following is correctly rewritten in **half the value** of the bar above? Circle the correct answer.

A

B

C

9. Look at the following bar.

Which of the following is correctly rewritten in **twice the value** of the bar above? Circle the correct answer.

10. Look at the following bar.

Which of the following is correctly rewritten in **half the value** of the bar above? Circle the correct answer.

A

B

C

Chapter 4
Grouping

1. Which bar is grouped correctly? Circle the correct answer.

2. Which bar is grouped correctly? Circle the correct answer.

3. Which bar is grouped correctly? Circle the correct answer.

4. Which bar is grouped correctly? Circle the correct answer.

5. Which bar is grouped correctly? Circle the correct answer.

A

B

C

6. Which bar is grouped correctly? Circle the correct answer.

A

B

C

7. Which bar is grouped correctly? Circle the correct answer.

8. Which bar is grouped correctly? Circle the correct answer.

9. Which bar is grouped correctly? Circle the correct answer.

10. Which bar is grouped correctly? Circle the correct answer.

Chapter 5
Rests

1. Which bar(s) is/ are having correct rests? Circle
   the correct answer(s).

2. Which bar(s) is/ are having correct rests? Circle
   the correct answer(s).

3. Which bar(s) is/ are having correct rests? Circle the correct answer(s).

4. Which bar(s) is/ are having correct rests? Circle the correct answer(s).

5. Which bar(s) is/ are having correct rests? Circle
   the correct answer(s).

A

B

C

D

6. Which bar(s) is/ are having correct rests? Circle
   the correct answer(s).

7. Which bar(s) is/ are having correct rests? Circle
   the correct answer(s).

8. Which bar(s) is/ are having correct rests? Circle
the correct answer(s).

A

B

C

D

Chapter 6
Concept of Note Values

1. Complete the following sentences by adding a number to each.

a) A breve is equal to _____ semiquavers.

b) A quaver is equal to _____ demisemiquavers.

c) In $\frac{12}{8}$, there are _____ dotted-crotchet beats in a bar.

d) In $\frac{9}{4}$, there are ___ dotted-minim beats in a bar.

e) A dotted crotchet is equal to _____ demisemiquavers.

f) In $\frac{9}{16}$, there are _____ dotted-semiquaver beats in a bar.

g) In $\frac{6}{8}$, $\overset{2}{\sqcap}$ is equal to ____ dotted crotchet(s).

h) In $\frac{4}{2}$, there are _____ minim beats in a bar.

i) A dotted semibreve is equal to _____ quavers.

2. Look at the following 'formulas' about note values and circle the correct ones.

A.   𝅘𝅥𝅮. + 𝅘𝅥.. = 𝅗𝅥.

B.   ♪. + ♪. = 𝅘𝅥.

C.   𝅘𝅥. + ♪ = 𝅗𝅥

D.   ‖𝅝‖ = 𝅝 + 𝅗𝅥. + 𝅘𝅥

E. $\overline{3}$ 𝅘𝅥 ♪ = 𝅘𝅥

F. $\overline{3}$ 𝅘𝅥 𝅘𝅥 𝅘𝅥 = 𝅗𝅥.

G.   ♪.. + ♪ = 𝅘𝅥

Chapter 7
Enharmonic equivalent

1. Which note is the correct enharmonic equivalent of this note? Circle the correct answer.

A

B

C

2. Which note is the correct enharmonic equivalent of this note? Circle the correct answer.

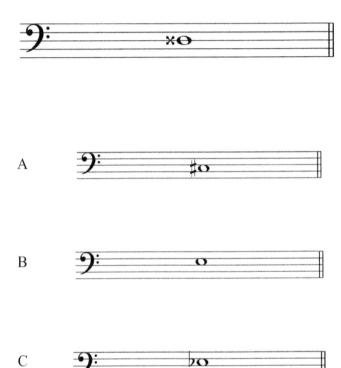

A

B

C

3. Which note is the correct enharmonic equivalent of this note? Circle the correct answer.

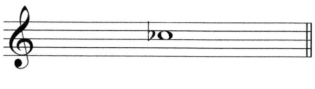

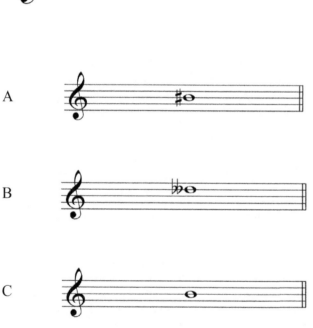

A

B

C

4. Which note is the correct enharmonic equivalent of this note? Circle the correct answer.

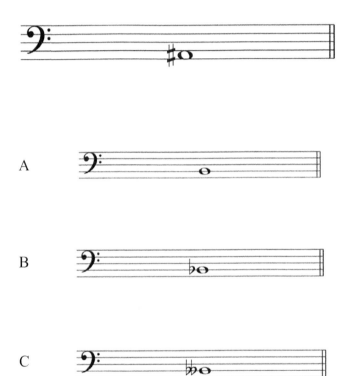

A

B

C

5. Which note is the correct enharmonic equivalent of this note? Circle the correct answer.

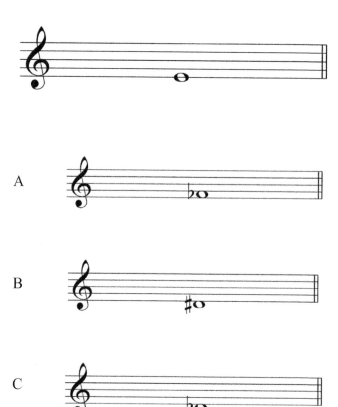

6. Which note is the correct enharmonic equivalent of this note? Circle the correct answer.

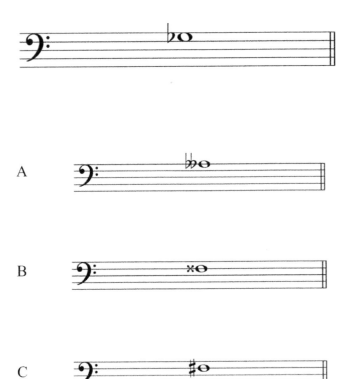

7. Which note is the correct enharmonic equivalent of this note? Circle the correct answer.

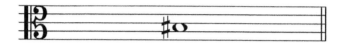

A

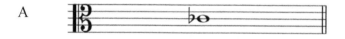

B

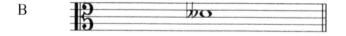

C

8. Which note is the correct enharmonic equivalent of this note? Circle the correct answer.

A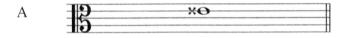

B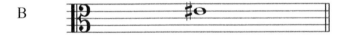

C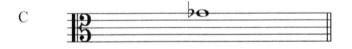

9. Which note is the correct enharmonic equivalent of this note? Circle the correct answer.

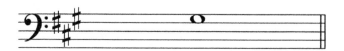

A

B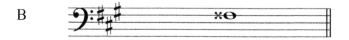

C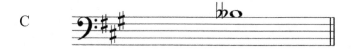

10. Which note is the correct enharmonic equivalent of this note? Circle the correct answer.

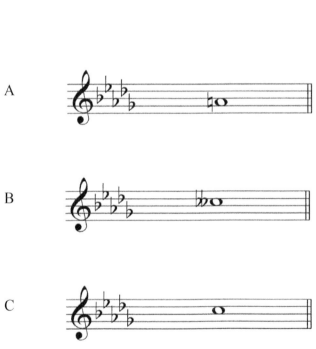

A

B

C

Chapter 8
Concept of Pitch

1. What is the name of this note? Tick (✓) one box to show the correct answer.

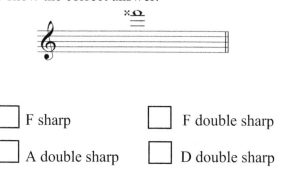

☐ F sharp   ☐ F double sharp

☐ A double sharp   ☐ D double sharp

2. What is the name of this note? Tick (✓) one box to show the correct answer.

☐ E flat   ☐ B flat

☐ G flat   ☐ A flat

3. What is the name of this note? Tick (✓) one box
   to show the correct answer.

☐ B double sharp   ☐ B sharp

☐ D double sharp   ☐ D sharp

4. What is the name of this note? Tick (✓) one box
   to show the correct answer.

☐ A sharp   ☐ G sharp

☐ F sharp   ☐ C sharp

5. What is the name of this note? Tick (✓) one box
    to show the correct answer.

☐ A sharp   ☐ B sharp

☐ C sharp   ☐ G sharp

6. What is the name of this note? Tick (✓) one box
    to show the correct answer.

☐ E flat   ☐ D flat

☐ F flat   ☐ C flat

7. What is the name of this note? Tick (✓) one box
    to show the correct answer.

☐ B flat   ☐ A flat

☐ G double flat   ☐ B double flat

8. What is the name of this note? Tick (✓) one box
    to show the correct answer.

☐ E flat   ☐ B flat

☐ D flat   ☐ C flat

9. What is the name of this note? Tick (✓) one box to show the correct answer.

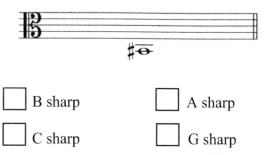

☐ B sharp   ☐ A sharp

☐ C sharp   ☐ G sharp

10. What is the name of this note? Tick (✓) one box to show the correct answer.

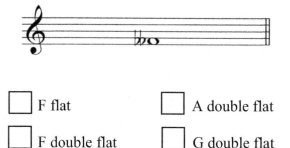

☐ F flat   ☐ A double flat

☐ F double flat   ☐ G double flat

11. What is the name of this note? Tick (✓) one box to show the correct answer.

☐ E double flat   ☐ C double flat

☐ B double flat   ☐ E flat

12. What is the name of this note? Tick (✓) one box to show the correct answer.

☐ F flat   ☐ E flat

☐ G flat   ☐ D flat

13. Rewrite the note in the given clef, keeping the pitch the same.

14. Rewrite the note in the given clef, keeping the pitch the same.

15. Rewrite the note in the given clef, keeping the pitch the same.

16. Rewrite the note in the given clef, keeping the pitch the same.

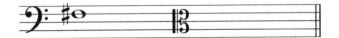

17. Rewrite the note in the given clef, keeping the pitch the same.

18. Rewrite the note in the given clef, keeping the pitch the same.

19. Rewrite the note in the given clef, keeping the pitch the same.

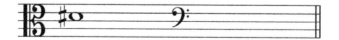

20. Rewrite the note in the given clef, keeping the pitch the same.

21. Compare bars X, Y and Z, then circle **True** or **False** for each of the two statements.

i)   Y and Z are at the same pitch.

True   **False**

ii) Y is one-octave lower than X.

True   **False**

22. Compare bars X, Y and Z, then circle **True** or **False** for each of the two statements.

i) X and Z are at the same pitch.

True **False**

ii) X is one-octave lower than Y.

True **False**

23. Compare bars X, Y and Z, then circle **True** or **False** for each of the two statements.

X

Y

Z

i) X and Y are at the same pitch.

True **False**

ii) Z is one-octave lower than Y.

True **False**

24. Compare bars X, Y and Z, then circle **True** or
    False for each of the two statements.

i)   Y and Z are at the same pitch.

True   **False**

ii) X is one-octave higher than Z.

True   **False**

25. Compare bars X, Y and Z, then circle **True** or **False** for each of the two statements.

i) X and Y are at the same pitch.

   True   **False**

ii) X is one-octave lower than Z.

   True   **False**

26. Compare bars X, Y and Z, then circle **True** or **False** for each of the two statements.

i)   Y and Z are at the same pitch.

True   **False**

ii)   X is one-octave higher than Y.

True   **False**

Chapter 9
Keys

1. Which is the correctly written key signature of C# minor? Circle the correct answer.

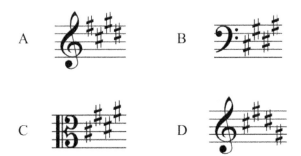

2. Which is the correctly written key signature of E♭ major? Circle the correct answer.

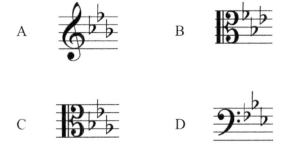

3. Which is the correctly written key signature of B major? Circle the correct answer.

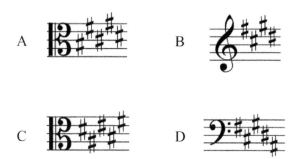

A   B

C   D

4. Which is the correctly written key signature of D♭ major? Circle the correct answer.

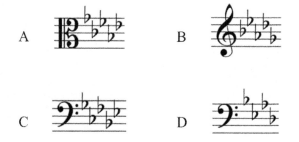

A   B

C   D

5. Which is the correctly written key signature of F# minor? Circle the correct answer.

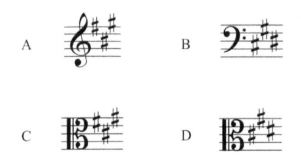

A   B

C   D

6. Which is the correctly written key signature of G minor? Circle the correct answer.

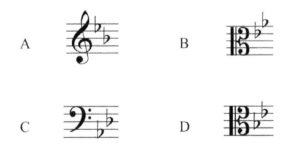

A   B

C   D

7. Which is the correctly written key signature of G#
minor? Circle the correct answer.

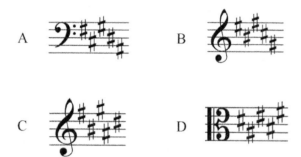

8. Which is the correctly written key signature of F
minor? Circle the correct answer.

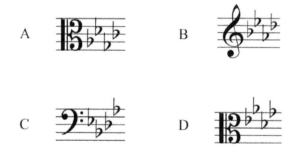

9. Which is the correct key of this melody? Circle the correct answer.

A major A minor E major C# minor

10. Which is the correct key of this melody? Circle the correct answer.

G minor B♭ major D minor F major

11. Which is the correct key of this melody? Circle the correct answer.

D major F# minor A major B minor

12. Which is the correct key of this melody? Circle the correct answer.

Eb major   F major   C minor   G minor

13. Which is the correct key of this melody? Circle the correct answer.

E major   B major   C# minor   F# minor

14. Which is the correct key of this melody? Circle the correct answer.

Db major   Ab major   F minor   Bb minor

15. Which is the correct key of this melody? Circle the correct answer.

Eb major   F minor   Ab major   Bb minor

16. Which is the correct key of this melody? Circle the correct answer.

E major   A major   B major   F# minor

17. Which is the correct key of this melody? Circle the correct answer.

E major   C# minor   B major   G# minor

18. Which is the correct key of this melody? Circle the correct answer.

Ab major   Db major   C minor   Bb minor

19. Which is the correct key of this melody? Circle the correct answer.

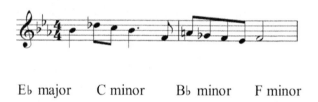

Eb major   C minor   Bb minor   F minor

20. Which is the correct key of this melody? Circle the correct answer.

B major   E major   C# minor   G# minor

21. Which is the correct key of this melody? Circle the correct answer.

A major   D major   F# minor   C# minor

22. Which is the correct key of this melody? Circle the correct answer.

Ab major   F minor   Bb major   Eb major

23. Which is the correct key of this melody? Circle the correct answer.

G major   G minor   E minor   F major

Chapter 10
Scales

1. Circle one note for X and one note for Y to show which notes are needed to complete the scale of F harmonic minor.

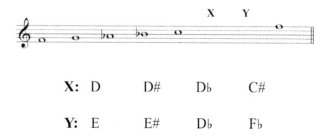

X: D D# D♭ C#

Y: E E# D♭ F♭

2. Circle one note for X and one note for Y to show which notes are needed to complete the scale of G# melodic minor.

X: F F# F♭ G♭

Y: E E# E♭ F#

3. Circle one note for X and one note for Y to show which notes are needed to complete the scale of Db major.

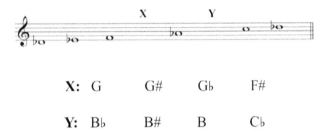

X: G G# Gb F#

Y: Bb B# B Cb

4. Circle one note for X and one note for Y to show which notes are needed to complete the scale of Eb major.

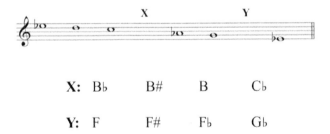

X: Bb B# B Cb

Y: F F# Fb Gb

5. Circle one note for X and one note for Y to show which notes are needed to complete the scale of C melodic minor.

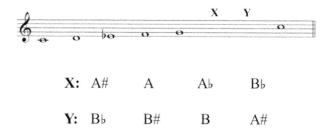

X: A#   A   Ab   Bb

Y: Bb   B#   B   A#

6. Circle one note for X and one note for Y to show which notes are needed to complete the scale of C# harmonic minor.

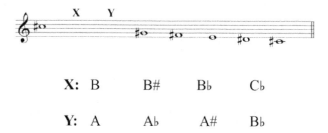

X: B   B#   Bb   Cb

Y: A   Ab   A#   Bb

7. Circle one note for X and one note for Y to show which notes are needed to complete the scale of Bb harmonic minor.

X: G# Gb G G#

Y: Ab A# A Bb

8. Circle one note for X and one note for Y to show which notes are needed to complete the scale of B major.

X: A# Ab A G#

Y: G Gb G# Ab

9. Circle one note for X and one note for Y to show which notes are needed to complete the scale of G# melodic minor.

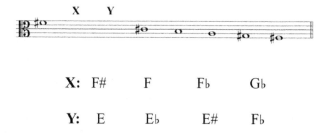

X: F#   F   F♭   G♭

Y: E   E♭   E#   F♭

10. Circle one note for X and one note for Y to show which notes are needed to complete the scale of C# melodic minor.

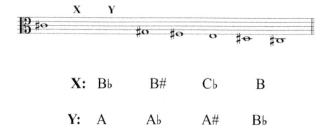

X: B♭   B#   C♭   B

Y: A   A♭   A#   B♭

11. Tick (✓) one box for the following named scale, to show which scale is correctly written.

A♭ major, descending

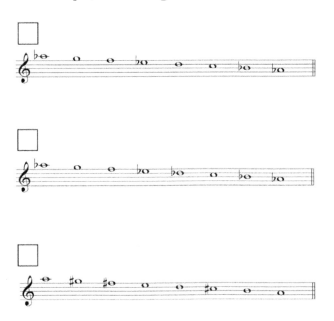

12. Tick (✓) one box for the following named scale, to show which scale is correctly written.

C# melodic minor, ascending

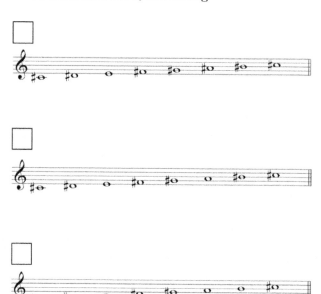

13. Tick (✓) one box for the following named scale, to show which scale is correctly written.

B♭ melodic minor, descending

14. Tick (✓) one box for the following named scale, to show which scale is correctly written.

B major, ascending

15. Tick (✓) one box for the following named scale, to show which scale is correctly written.

Db major, ascending

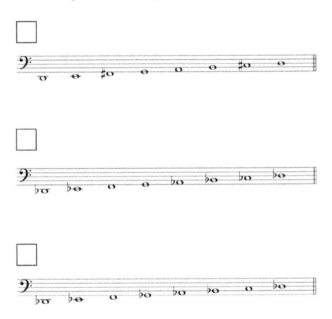

16. Tick (✓) one box for the following named scale,
    to show which scale is correctly written.

C melodic minor, ascending

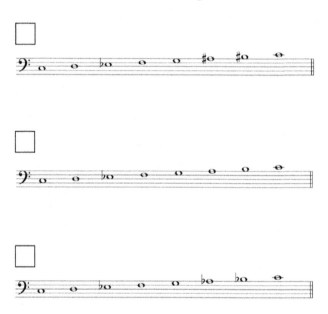

17. Tick (✓) one box for the following named scale, to show which scale is correctly written.

E major, descending

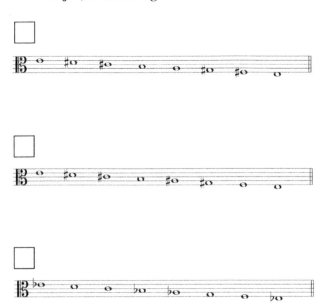

18. Tick (✓) one box for the following named scale, to show which scale is correctly written.

F harmonic minor, ascending

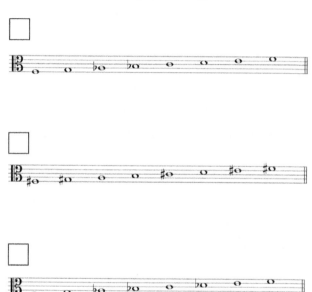

19. Tick (✓) one box for the following named scale, to show which scale is correctly written.

B harmonic minor, descending

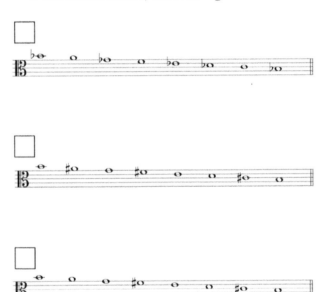

20. Tick (✓) one box for the following named scale, to show which scale is correctly written.

G# harmonic minor, ascending

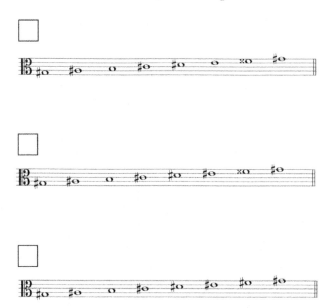

Circle True or False for each statement.

21. This is correctly written chromatic scale beginning on E.

True   **False**

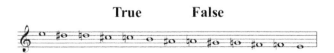

22. This is correctly written chromatic scale beginning on B#.

True   **False**

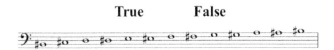

23. This is correctly written chromatic scale beginning on G#.

True   **False**

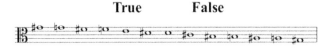

24. This is correctly written chromatic scale beginning on D♭.

True   **False**

25. Look at the following scale:

Circle True or False for each of the following statements about this scale.

a) This is the correctly written scale of C# harmonic minor, ascending.

True   **False**

b) The largest interval between two notes next to each other is an augmented 2nd.

True   **False**

c) There are three pairs of semitones in this scale.

True   **False**

d) The submediant is E.

True   **False**

26. Look at the following scale:

Circle True or False for each of the following statements about this scale.

a) This is the correctly written scale of F# melodic minor, descending.

True   **False**

b) The largest interval between two notes next to each other is a major 2nd.

True   **False**

c) There are two pairs of semitones in this scale.

True   **False**

d) The subdominant is B.

True   **False**

27. Look at the following scale:

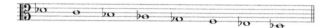

Circle True or False for each of the following statements about this scale.

a) This is the correctly written scale of Db major, descending.

True   **False**

b) The largest interval between two notes next to each other is a major 2nd.

True   **False**

c) There are three pairs of semitones in this scale.

True   **False**

d) The mediant is Bb.

True   **False**

28. Look at the following scale:

Circle True or False for each of the following statements about this scale.

a) This is the correctly written scale of B♭ melodic minor, descending.

True   **False**

b) The largest interval between two notes next to each other is an augmented 2nd.

True   **False**

c) There are two pairs of semitones in this scale.

True   **False**

d) The dominant is E♭.

True   **False**

Chapter 11
Technical Names

Circle True or False for each statement.

1. This is the dominant note in G minor.

True   **False**

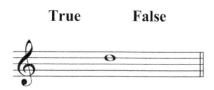

2. This is the supertonic note in B ♭ major.

True   **False**

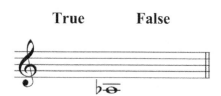

3. This is the submediant note in C minor.

True   **False**

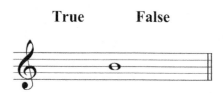

4. This is the subdominant note in G# minor.

True   **False**

5. This is the mediant note in F minor.

True   **False**

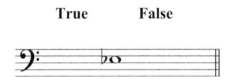

6. This is the submediant note in A ♭ major.

True   **False**

7. This is the leading note in E minor.

True   **False**

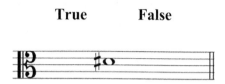

8. This is the subdominant note in D ♭ major.

True   **False**

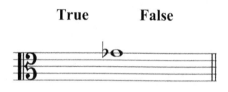

9. This is the tonic note in C major.

True   **False**

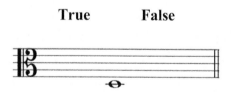

Chapter 12
Intervals

1. Circle the type of the following interval.

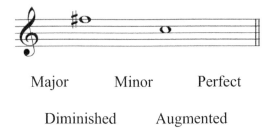

Major   Minor   Perfect

Diminished   Augmented

2. Circle the type of the following interval.

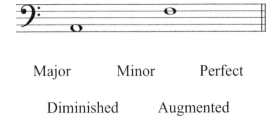

Major   Minor   Perfect

Diminished   Augmented

3. Circle the type of the following interval.

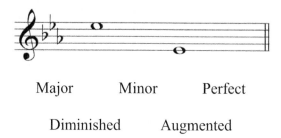

Major   Minor   Perfect

Diminished   Augmented

4. Circle the type of the following interval.

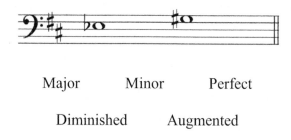

Major   Minor   Perfect

Diminished   Augmented

5. Circle the type of the following interval.

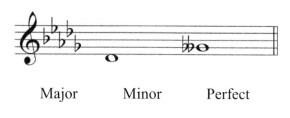

Major   Minor   Perfect

Diminished   Augmented

6. Circle the type of the following interval.

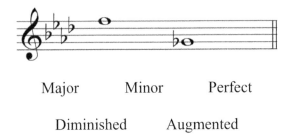

Major   Minor   Perfect

Diminished   Augmented

7. Circle the type of the following interval.

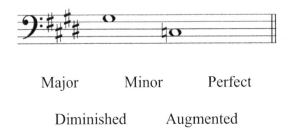

Major   Minor   Perfect

Diminished   Augmented

8. Circle the type of the following interval.

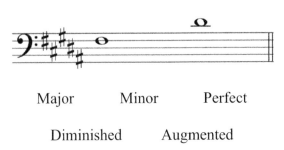

Major   Minor   Perfect

Diminished   Augmented

9. Circle the type of the following interval.

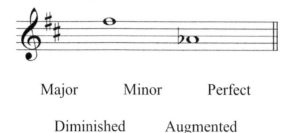

Major   Minor   Perfect

Diminished   Augmented

10. Circle the type of the following interval.

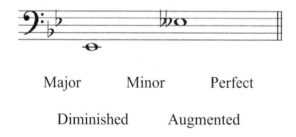

Major   Minor   Perfect

Diminished   Augmented

11. Circle the type of the following interval.

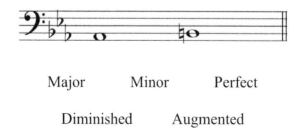

Major   Minor   Perfect

Diminished   Augmented

12. Circle the type of the following interval.

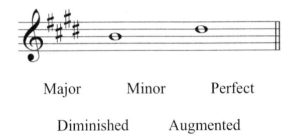

Major   Minor   Perfect

Diminished   Augmented

13. Circle the type of the following interval.

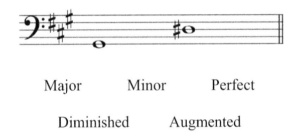

Major   Minor   Perfect

Diminished   Augmented

14. Circle the type of the following interval.

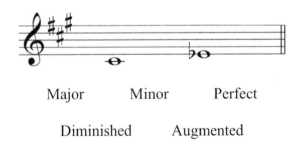

Major   Minor   Perfect

Diminished   Augmented

15. Write notes to form the named intervals.
The note you write should be higher than the given note.

Perfect 4th

16. Write notes to form the named intervals.
The note you write should be higher than the given note.

Diminished 5th

17. Write notes to form the named intervals.
The note you write should be higher than the given note.

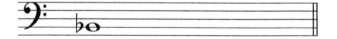

Minor 6th

18. Write notes to form the named intervals.
    The note you write should be higher than the given note.

Diminished 8ve

19. Write notes to form the named intervals.
    The note you write should be higher than the given note.

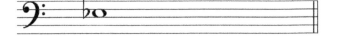

Major 7th

20. Write notes to form the named intervals.
    The note you write should be higher than the given note.

Minor 3rd

21. Write notes to form the named intervals.
The note you write should be higher than the given note.

Augmented 5th

22. Write notes to form the named intervals.
The note you write should be higher than the given note.

Diminished 3rd

23. Write notes to form the named intervals.
The note you write should be higher than the given note.

Perfect 4th

24. Write notes to form the named intervals.
    The note you write should be higher than the given note.

Major 6th

25. Write notes to form the named intervals.
    The note you write should be higher than the given note.

Perfect 5th

26. Write notes to form the named intervals.
    The note you write should be higher than the given note.

Minor 2nd

Chapter 13
Triads and Chords

1. Circle True or False for each of the following statements.

a) This is the tonic triad in F major.

True   **False**

b) This is the dominant triad in A ♭ major.

True   **False**

c) This is the dominant triad in E major.

True   **False**

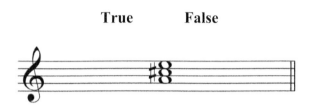

d) This is the subdominant triad in A major.

True   **False**

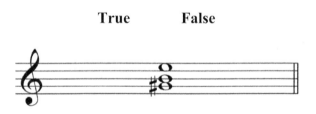

e) This is the tonic triad in C# minor.

True   **False**

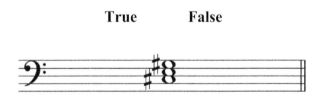

f) This is the tonic triad in B major.

True   **False**

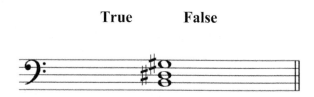

g) This is the subdominant triad in A ♭ major.

True   **False**

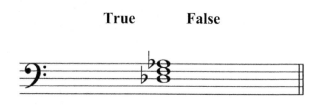

h) This is the dominant triad in B ♭ minor.

True   **False**

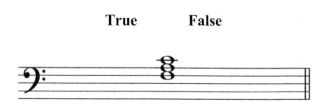

i) This is the tonic triad in D minor.

True   **False**

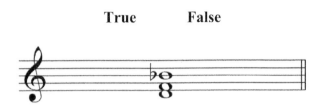

j) This is the subdominant triad in G minor.

True   **False**

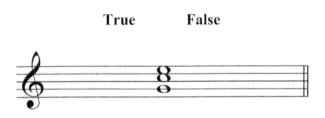

k) This is the tonic triad in G minor.

True   **False**

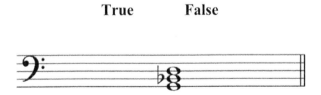

l) This is the subdominant triad in A minor.

True   **False**

m) This is the dominant triad in D major.

True   **False**

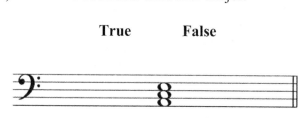

n) This is the subdominant triad in E ♭ major.

True   **False**

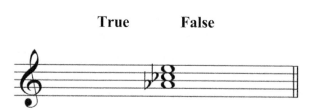

o) This is the dominant triad in F minor.

True   **False**

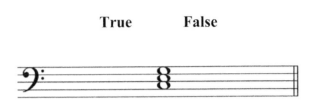

p) This is the tonic triad in B major.

True   **False**

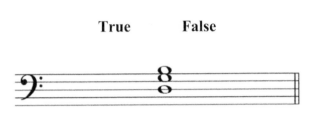

q) This is the dominant triad in E ♭ major.

True   **False**

2. Name each of these triads by writing either I, IV
   or V in the boxes underneath.

a)   D major

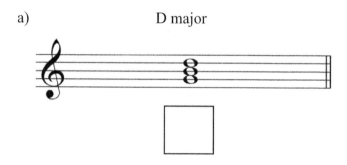

b)   D ♭ major

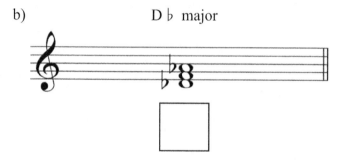

c)   E major

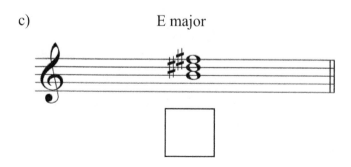

d)   G minor

e)   G minor

f)   B ♭ minor

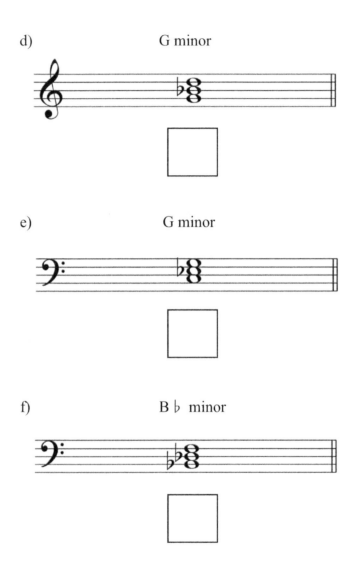

g) A♭ major

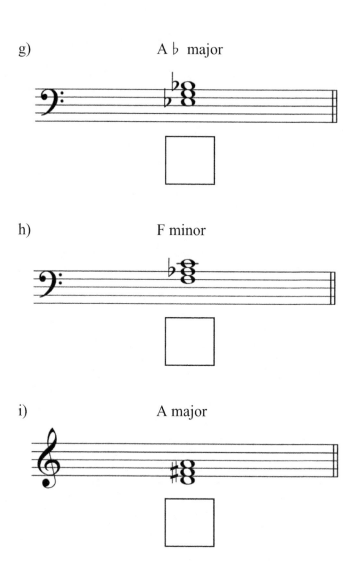

h) F minor

i) A major

j)   A minor

k)   E minor

l)   F# minor

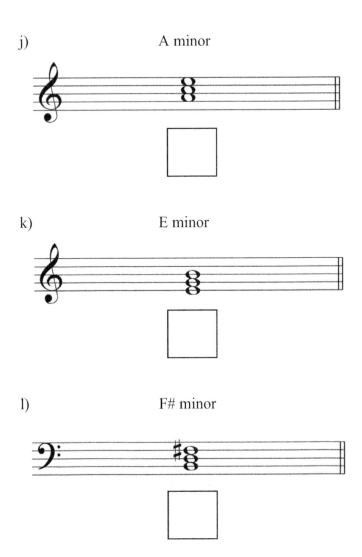

m)   F minor

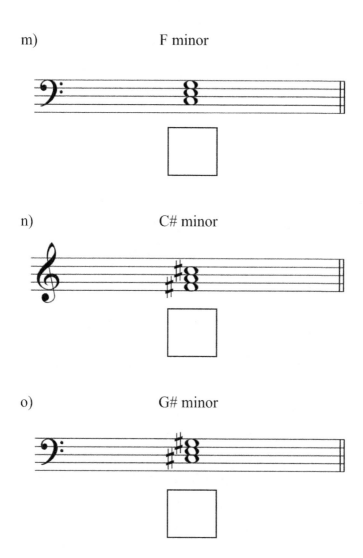

n)   C# minor

o)   G# minor

3. Write either I, IV or V in each of the boxes underneath this extract to name each chord. The key is A major.

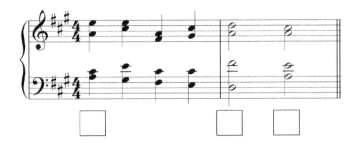

4. Write either I, IV or V in each of the boxes underneath this extract to name each chord. The key is C minor.

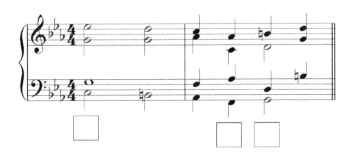

5. Write either I, IV or V in each of the boxes underneath this extract to name each chord. The key is B ♭ major.

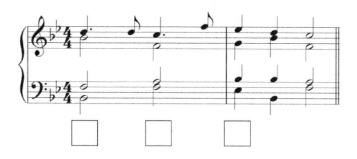

6. Write either I, IV or V in each of the boxes underneath this extract to name each chord. The key is C minor.

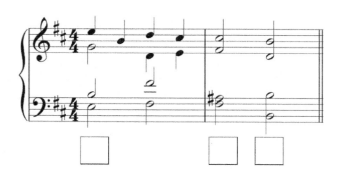

Chapter 14
Terms, Signs and Instruments

I. Concepts about instruments and voices
Circle True or False for each of the following statements.

a)   The clarinet is a brass instrument.

        True   False

b)   The trombone is the lowest-sounding brass instrument.

        True   False

c)   The tambourine produce sounds of indefinite pitch.

        True   False

d)   The flute is the highest-sounding woodwind instrument.

        True   False

e)   The oboe is a single-reed instrument.

        True   False

f)   The clarinet is a brass instrument.

        True   False

g) The trumpet is a double-reed instrument.

True   False

h) The violin is the highest-sounding string instrument.

True   False

i) The horn can be played 'pizzicato'.

True   False

j) The cello is the lowest-sounding string instrument.

True   False

k) The tuba is a brass instrument.

True   False

l) The double bass uses the alto clef sometimes.

True   False

m) The clarinet is a transposing instrument.

True   False

n) The viola is a non-transposing instrument.

        True   False

o) The viola uses the alto clef most of the time.

        True   False

p) The bassoon is the lowest-sounding woodwind instrument.

        True   False

q) The horn is the highest-sounding brass instrument.

        True   False

r) The oboe is a transposing instrument.

        True   False

s) The highest male voice type is called tenor.

        True   False

t) The lowest female voice type is called bass.

        True   False

u) The voice type between tenor and bass is
    called alto.

            True   False

v) The lowest male voice type is called baritone.

            True   False

w) The mezzo-soprano voice has a higher range
    than an alto voice.

            True   False

x) '*una corda*' means to pluck.

            True   False

y) '*arco*' means to play with the bow.

            True   False

z) The violin player may be asked to play
    " *sul G* " sometimes.
            True   False

II. Terms and Signs
Circle the correct answers.

a) The following sign means:

    A. down bow
    B. up bow
    C. pause on the note
    D. detached

b) The following sign means:

    A. detached
    B. accented
    C. slightly separated
    D. smoothly

c) The term that has a similar meaning to **adagio** is:

    A. allegretto
    B. lent
    C. moderato
    D. vivace

d) The term that has a similar meaning to **douce** is:

    A. allargando
    B. deciso
    C. diminuendo
    D. dolce

e) The term that has a similar meaning to **stringendo** is:

    A. diminuendo
    B. crescendo
    C. accelerando
    D. ritardando

f) **rubato** means:

    A. with some freedom of time
    B. as fast as possible
    C. the same speed
    D. in strict time

g) **grazioso** means:

    A. as soft as possible
    B. playfully
    C. gracefully
    D. getting faster

h) **retenu** means:

    A. bold
    B. rhythmically
    C. with some freedom of time
    D. held back

i) **allegro assai** means:

    A. very slow
    B. very fast
    C. getting slower
    D. getting faster

j) **mesto** means:

    A. moderately
    B. slower
    C. accented
    D. sad

k) **maestoso** means:

    A. slower
    B. majestic
    C. in strict time
    D. with feeling

l) *leggiero* means:

    A. light
    B. heavy
    C. energetic
    D. rather slow

m) **modéré** means:

    A. lively
    B. slow
    C. sad
    D. moderately

n) **con brio** means:

    A. with mute
    B. lively
    C. getting slower
    D. with movement

o) *deciso* means:

    A. with movement
    B. with determination
    C. with mute
    D. sweet, soft

p) *sf* means:

    A. loud, then immediately soft
    B. forced, accented
    C. detached
    D. held back

q) **adagietto** means:

    A. broadening
    B. slow
    C. rather slow
    D. very slow

r) **misterioso** means:

    A. in a military style
    B. in a singing style
    C. in the style of a march
    D. in a mysterious mood

s) *come prima* means:

    A. as before
    B. gradually getting faster
    C. gradually getting slower
    D. playful

t)   *sub. **p*** means:

   A.   gradually getting softer
   B.   very soft
   C.   as soft as possible
   D.   suddenly soft

u)   **sostenuto** means:

   A.   slower
   B.   sustained
   C.   soft
   D.   in an undertone

v)   **amabile** means:

   A.   fast
   B.   slow
   C.   pleasant
   D.   with feeling

w)   **sempre** means:

   A.   suddenly
   B.   as, similar to
   C.   as above
   D.   always

x) **più** means:

    A. more
    B. little
    C. but
    D. again

y) **tranquillo** means:

    A. lively
    B. tenderly
    C. sad
    D. calm

z) **D.C.** means:

    A. the end
    B. repeat from the beginning
    C. as before
    D. in the same way

III. Ornaments

1. What is the name of the ornament used in the following bar? Circle the correct answer.

   A. turn
   B. trill
   C. lower mordent
   D. upper mordent

2. What is the name of the ornament used in the following bar? Circle the correct answer.

   A. turn
   B. appoggiatura
   C. acciaccatura
   D. upper mordent

3. What is the name of the ornament used in the following bar? Circle the correct answer.

  A. turn
  B. appoggiatura
  C. acciaccatura
  D. trill

4. What is the name of the ornament used in the following bar? Circle the correct answer.

  A. acciaccatura
  B. appoggiatura
  C. upper mordent
  D. lower mordent

5. What is the name of the ornament used in the following bar? Circle the correct answer.

   A.   turn
   B.   upper mordent
   C.   lower mordent
   D.   trill

6. What is the name of the ornament used in the following bar? Circle the correct answer.

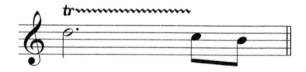

   A.   trill
   B.   turn
   C.   upper mordent
   D.   lower mordent

Answers

Chapter 1
Time Signatures

1. $\mathbf{C}$ 2. $\frac{9}{8}$ 3. $\frac{4}{2}$

4. $\frac{12}{16}$ 5. $\frac{3}{4}$ 6. $\frac{6}{8}$

7. $\frac{12}{8}$ 8. $\frac{6}{4}$ 9. $\frac{9}{4}$

10. $\frac{9}{16}$

Chapter 2
Shift between simple time and compound time.

1. B	2. C	3. B	4. C	5. A
6. B	7. C	8. A	9. B	10. A

Chapter 3
Rewrite a bar of notes:
twice the value or half the value

1. A	2. B	3. C	4. B	5. C
6. A	7. B	8. B	9. C	10. A

Chapter 4
Grouping

1. C	2. A	3. A	4. B	5. A
6. C	7. C	8. B	9. A	10. C

Chapter 5
Rests

1. A, B	2. C, D	3. B	4. A, B, C
5. D	6. B, C	7. A, B, D	8. C

Chapter 6
Concept of Note Values
1.

a) 32	b) 4	c) 4	d) 3	e) 12
f) 3	g) 1	h) 4	i) 12	

2. B, C, D, E, G

Chapter 7
Enharmonic equivalent

1. C   2. B   3. C   4. B   5. A
6. C   7. B   8. B   9. A   10. B

Chapter 8
Concept of Pitch

1. F double sharp   2. G flat
3. D double sharp   4. A sharp
5. G sharp   6. E flat
7. B double flat   8. C flat
9. B sharp   10. F double flat
11. B double flat   12. F flat
13.

14.

15.

(cont. Chapter 8)

16.

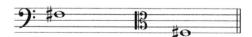

17.

18.

19.

20.

(cont. Chapter 8)

21. i) False	ii) True
22. i) True	ii) True
23. i) True	ii) False
24. i) False	ii) False
25. i) False	ii) True
26. i) True	ii) True

Chapter 9
Keys

1. A   2. C   3. D   4. B
5. C   6. D   7. A   8. B
9. A major   10. F major   11. B minor
12. C minor   13. B major   14. B♭ minor
15. F minor   16. E major   17. C# minor
18. D♭ major   19. B♭ minor   20. G# minor
21. F# minor   22. A♭ major   23. G minor

Chapter 10
Scales

1. X: D♭   Y: E
2. X: F#   Y: E
3. X: G♭   Y: B♭
4. X: B♭   Y: F
5. X: A   Y: B
6. X: B#   Y: A
7. X: G♭   Y: A
8. X: A#   Y: G#
9. X: F#   Y: E
10. X: B   Y: A
11.

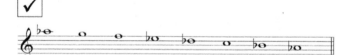

12.

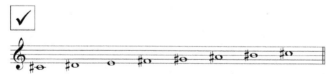

(cont. Chapter 10)

13.

14.

15.

16.

(cont. Chapter 10)

17.

18.

19.

20.

(cont. Chapter 10)

21. True	22. False	23. False	24. True
25. a) True	b) True	c) True	d) False
26. a) False	b) False	c) False	d) True
27. a) True	b) True	c) False	d) False
28. a) True	b) False	c) True	d) False

Chapter 11
Technical Names

1. True	2. False	3. False	4. True
5. False	6. True	7. True	8. True
9. False			

Chapter 12
Intervals

1. Augmented	2. Minor	3. Perfect
4. Augmented	5. Diminished	6. Major
7. Augmented	8. Major	9. Augmented
10. Diminished	11. Augmented	12. Major
13. Perfect	14. Diminished	
15.		

(cont. Chapter 12)

16.

17.

18.

19.

20.

(cont. Chapter 12)

21.

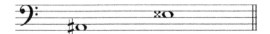

22.

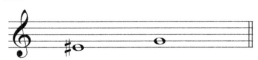

23.

24.

25.

(cont. Chapter 12)

26.

Chapter 13
Triads and Chords

1. a) False   b) False   c) False
   d) False   e) True   f) False
   g) True   h) True   i) False
   j) False   k) True   l) True
   m) False   n) False   o) True
   p) False   q) True

2. a) IV   b) I   c) V
   d) I   e) IV   f) I
   g) V   h) I   i) IV
   j) I   k) I   l) IV
   m) V   n) IV   o) IV

(cont. Chapter 13)

3.

4.

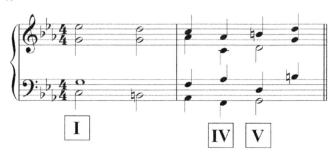

5.

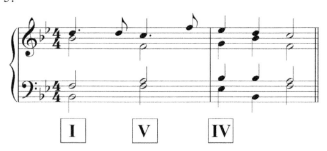

(cont. Chapter 13)

6.

Chapter 14
Terms, Signs and Instruments
I.

a) False	b) False	c) True	d) True
e) False	f) False	g) False	h) True
i) False	j) False	k) True	l) False
m) True	n) True	o) True	p) True
q) False	r) False	s) True	t) False
u) False	v) False	w) True	x) False
y) True	z) True		

(cont. Chapter 14)

II.

1.

a) B	b) C	c) B	d) D	e) C
f) A	g) C	h) D	i) B	j) D
k) B	l) A	m) D	n) B	o) B
p) B	q) C	r) D	s) A	t) D
u) B	v) C	w) D	x) A	y) D
z) B				

III.

1. D   2. C   3. A   4. B   5. C   6. A

For more music resources, please visit: www.reginapratley.com

Thank you!

Printed in Great Britain
by Amazon